Off to prison. An engraving from G. A. Sala, 'Twice Round the Clock', first published in 1859. Sala wrote of the vehicle: 'By some it is called "Her Majesty's Carriage", from the fact that the crown and the initials "V.R." are painted on the panels. More far-fetched wags call it "Long Tom's Coffin". The police and the reporters, for shortness, call it "The Van".' The term 'Black Maria', in use by the end of the century, is of American origin, having been current in Boston since the 1840s. Sala described the 'great black, shining, cellular omnibus' as 'a prison on wheels, a peripatetic penitentiary, a locomotive hulk'.

Victorian and Edwardian Prisons

Trevor May

CONTENTS

ACKNOWLEDGEMENTS
Illustrations are acknowledged as follows: Cambridge and County Folk Museum, pages 8–9 (top); the Governor, HM Young Offenders' Institution, Portland, pages 31, 39; Cadbury Lamb, pages 19 (bottom), 20 (bottom), 30 (top); Timothy Millett, page 23 (bottom). Other illustrations are from the author's collection or from the source stated in the caption.

Cover: *The interior of Montgomery county gaol, c. 1875. Photograph reproduced by kind permission of the Powysland Museum.*

British Library Cataloguing in Publication Data: May, Trevor. Victorian and Edwardian Prisons. – (Shire Library; 450) 1. Prisons – Great Britain – History – 19th century. 2. Prisons – Great Britain – History – 20th century. I. Title 365.9'41'09034. ISBN-13: 978 0 7478 0641 7.

Published by Shire Publications Ltd,
PO Box 883, Oxford, OX1 9PL, UK • PO Box 3985, New York, NY 10185-3985, USA
Email: shire@shirebooks.co.uk • www.shirebooks.co.uk
© 2006 by Trevor May.
First published 2006.
Transferred to digital print on demand 2014.
Shire Library 450. ISBN-13: 978 0 74780 641 7.
Trevor May is hereby identified as the author of this work in accordance with Section 77 of the Copyright, Designs and Patents Act 1988.

Printed and bound in Great Britain.

Shire Publications is supporting the Woodland Trust, the UK's leading woodland conservation charity, by funding the dedication of trees.

THE SWEEP OF PRISON HISTORY

At the beginning of the twenty-first century the United Kingdom had around 150 prisons, ranging from state-of-the-art, new buildings to ones originally constructed two hundred years ago or earlier. It was in the nineteenth century that prisons as we would recognise them came into existence and were forged into a national system administered by the central government.

Throughout history those who do not conform to certain social values have been removed from society. This has taken the form of ostracism or 'sending to Coventry' at one end of the spectrum, and to the final and irreversible employment of execution at the other. In Britain, outlawry and banishment were favoured methods in the Middle Ages. In the seventeenth century transportation to overseas colonies was introduced. Not until the nineteenth century did imprisonment become the norm.

Prisons had, nevertheless, existed much earlier. In 1166 the Assize of Clarendon had laid it down that there should be a prison in every county, but their function was not so much to punish offenders as to confine them *before* trial. Then, as judges made the rounds of their circuits, prisoners would be presented by writ of 'general gaol delivery' at the assize courts. Punishment tended to take other forms: fine, mutilation (as a visible warning to others) and, in the earliest times, slavery (a severe but practicable form of 'victim support'). Prisons themselves existed in some variety. Apart from the secular county prisons, there were those granted by charter to particular towns or corporations. The church had its prisons, ranging from monastic prisons for refractory monks to prisons run by bishops. The Bishop of Winchester, for example, had a small prison – The Clink – on lands that he possessed in Southwark, which passed into the language as an epithet for 'gaol'.

Newgate in 1772. Newgate was one of the gates in the Roman wall surrounding London. A prison stood here from at least the twelfth century, perhaps earlier. The novelist Henry Fielding, a London magistrate, described the London prisons (of which Newgate was the most notorious example) as a 'prototype of hell'. Despite this, the exterior of Newgate, before it was rebuilt between 1770 and 1778, gave little indication of the horrors within. The windmill on the roof was installed by Stephen Hales in 1752 to assist ventilation, and to mitigate the effects of 'gaol fever'.

THE TOWER OF LONDON

WHITE TOWER

BYWARD TOWER

STAIRCASE WHITE TOWER

PASSAGE IN BLOODY TOWER

ST JOHN'S CHAPEL

LANE

BLOODY TOWER

BELL TOWER

BEAUVER TOWER

W.H. PRIOR del.

TRAITORS GATE

BYWARD TOWER

For centuries the Tower of London was the principal royal palace in the capital, and at times it housed the Mint, the Royal Observatory and a menagerie. It was also the place of incarceration for prisoners of state. During the First World War eleven spies were executed by firing squad in the outer ward, while during the Second World War Rudolf Hess was imprisoned there for a short while.

From this amorphous mass the modern prison system emerged as Parliament passed legislation to reform administration and conditions, or to implement new penal theories. Two words of warning are justified, however. First, legislation can be a poor guide to what actually happened, for laws were often implemented (or failed to be implemented) in ways that the legislators had not foreseen. Those responsible for putting laws into effect might be obstructive, for reform often required additional expenditure that they were reluctant to undertake. Likewise, those responsible for implementing the law within the prisons themselves had

The architect Robert Smirke reconstructed Lincoln Castle Gaol between 1823 and 1830. Around twenty Victorian prisons were contained within castles, including York Castle County Gaol, Dover Gaol, and Norwich and Oxford County Gaols.

their own opinions and were sometimes inclined to let new ideas wash over their heads: Major H. S. Rogers, Surveyor of Prisons, lamented in 1910 that 'in prison work outside opinions of faddists and others have to be reckoned with'. Second, prison history should not be seen as a story of continuous and inevitable progress, or of a steady growth of humane attitudes towards prisoners. For example, 'slopping out' (the daily ritual of cleaning the buckets used by prisoners

The idea of the castle as prison lingered in the imagination and found architectural expression in a number of establishments. Buckingham Borough Gaol was built in 1748 after a fire in the town some twenty years before and the return of the Summer Assizes from Aylesbury to Buckingham the previous year. The rounded front was added in 1839 to provide accommodation for the chief constable of the Buckingham Borough Police Force. Closed after the passage of the 1877 Prison Act, it had a chequered history as police cells, fire station, public toilets and café until it was opened as a museum in 1993.

The Fleet Prison in London was first recorded in 1170–1. Rebuilt after the Great Fire, and again in the 1780s after having been burnt down in the Gordon Riots, it was closed in 1842 and demolished four years later. Many of the inmates were imprisoned for debt. Prisoners were required to pay for their lodgings, and those who had no other means were compelled to beg at 'the grate', which fronted Farringdon Street. At Exeter's Southgate Gaol a boot on a string was always left hanging from an upper storey overlooking the street – perhaps the origin of the expression 'living on a shoestring'.

as toilets while confined in their cells at night) was one of the great indignities of twentieth-century prisons, yet it seems to have dated only from about the 1870s. It developed as the water-closets regularly installed in cells from the 1840s became unusable as a result of clogging and burst pipes and were not replaced. Other things have come round in a circular manner (albeit in a modern form). Privately managed prisons were a bane of the eighteenth century but were reintroduced in the 1990s. Even the hulks (prison ships) that were a feature of early-Victorian England were reincarnated in 1997, when HMP (Her Majesty's Prison) *Weare* was moored in Portland Harbour (where it was closed in 2005).

EIGHTEENTH-CENTURY PRISON REFORM

It is simplistic to suppose that the Victorian era began in 1837 when the Queen came to the throne. Indeed, many historians have argued that it was in the half-century before Victoria's accession that many 'Victorian' attitudes were formed. This was a period of rapid industrialisation, accompanied by vast economic and social change. Many of the old restraints were breaking down as rural society gradually gave way to one dominated by the towns. It is hardly surprising, therefore, that many members of the middle and upper classes sought to exert 'social control' over the emerging working class, although this is not a term that they would have used. Attempts were made across a range of social issues, from the poor law to prisons, to mould the lower orders, and to impose on them the values of those higher up in the social hierarchy. The state came to intervene more and more in the lives of ordinary people. Rather than the spectacular but infrequent intervention of the criminal law typified by the gallows, the law (enforced by new police forces after 1829) came to permeate people's lives, and the prison became its prime agent.

During the last two decades of the eighteenth century there was something of a prison-building boom in Britain. A number of factors drove this activity. First, the independence of the American colonies removed a reservoir into which convicts could be poured, and some forty thousand had been shipped there by 1776. It was not until 1787 that the so-called 'First Fleet' set sail for New South Wales with 778 convicts on board. Second, the outbreak of war with France produced a need to house prisoners of war in great numbers – between 1793 and 1815 over 122,000 prisoners of war were detained (compared with sixteen thousand prisoners in civil prisons in 1816). As this was seen as a temporary problem, permanent solutions were not generally sought. Instead, prisoners were housed in camps, such as that at Norman Cross in Cambridgeshire, or on hulks, while the officers were often paroled. Some permanent buildings were erected,

The chain room at Millbank Penitentiary. By the time Henry Mayhew and John Binny visited the prison in the early 1860s many of these restraints had become obsolete. Some eighteenth-century prisons were so dilapidated that heavy leg-irons were a cheap substitute for building repairs.

Before 1826 there were over two hundred capital offences in Britain; thereafter only treason, arson, piracy and murder carried the death penalty. Public hangings were not abolished until 1866, after which date executions took place privately inside prisons. A public hanging was the pretext for the publication and sale of broadsheets, such as this from the collection of the Cambridge and County Folk Museum, often containing what purported to be the confession and dying words of the offender. Lucas and Reader were hanged outside Cambridge County Gaol on 13th April 1850. Notice the misprinting of 'Gaol' and the gallows crudely added to a printer's block of prison gates.

THE DYING

Elias Lu

Who were Executed this mor

the most notable being Dartmoor, which received its first prisoners in 1809. Another was at Perth in Scotland, vestiges of which still survive in HMP Perth.

The third stimulus to the building of prisons came from the work of reformers such as John Howard (1726?–90). Early-eighteenth-century prisons left much scope for reform. It was common practice for prisons to be run for profit by the gaoler, who charged fees from the inmates. These applied to such things as the provision of food and bedding, light and fuel, or transfer to better accommodation. That attempts were made by Parliament from the fourteenth to the eighteenth century to regulate the practice simply demonstrates how intractable was the problem. Prisoners also exacted their toll on newcomers. One practice particularly prevalent in debtors' prisons was the extortion of 'chummage' or 'garnish', sometimes referred to as 'letting the black dog walk'. A slang dictionary of 1811 described chummage as: 'Money paid by the richer sort of prisoners … to the poorer, for their share of a room. When prisons are very full, which is too often the case … two or three prisoners are obliged to sleep in a room. A prisoner who can pay for being alone, chuses [sic] two poor chums, who for a stipulated price, called chummage, give up their share of the room, and sleep on the stairs, or as the term is, ruff it.'

Overcrowding led to disease, and gaol fever (probably epidemic typhus) was a serious problem. In 1782 three times as many prisoners died of gaol fever at

Elizabeth Fry (1780–1845) was a prominent Quaker reformer who turned her attention to many social problems other than prisons, for which she is most famous. In 1817 she founded the Ladies' Association for the Reformation of Female Prisoners in Newgate. In the 1820s she campaigned for the improvement of conditions for female transportees, securing the abolition of leg-irons, stay of sentence for nursing mothers until the baby was weaned, and provision for children under seven to accompany their mother. It is more difficult to assess her impact on prisoners themselves. Commentators were fulsome in their praise. The American ambassador, after seeing Mrs Fry in Newgate, claimed that 'the wretched outcasts have been tamed and subdued by [her] Christian eloquence', but we have no accounts from the prisoners themselves.

os and **CONFESSION** OF

s AND **Mary Reader,**

il 13)   in front of the County Goal at Cambridge, for the wilful MURDER of SUSAN LUCAS.

In 1845 the 'Illustrated London News' described the hulk 'Warrior', moored on the river Thames at Woolwich, as 'not altogether an unpicturesque riverside object'. The six hundred prisoners housed there probably thought otherwise. About 120 convicts of the best character were housed on the upper deck in the 'galleries', shown here. The prisoners worked at heavy labour on the river or in the arsenal. The engraving of 1862 shows them scraping shot. (Illustrations from the 'Illustrated London News', 21st February 1846, and Henry Mayhew and John Binny, 'The Criminal Prisons of London', 1862)

Above: *Built at Princetown, on one of the bleakest parts of Dartmoor, the prison of that name was constructed at the beginning of the nineteenth century to house French prisoners of war. Later used to incarcerate American prisoners during the war of 1812, it became surplus to requirements and was closed down. Reopened in 1850 as a convict prison, its popular notoriety in Victorian times was prodigious, yet for much of that period it was classified for the confinement of invalid convicts.*

Left: *Jeremy Bentham (1748–1832), philosopher and penal reformer. With his idea of the panopticon, Bentham contributed much to the thinking on prison architecture. In addition, his views on utilitarianism, with its suggestion that people are motivated solely by their desire to seek pleasurable or avoid painful experiences, contributed a psychological basis for much penal reform.*

Gentlemen debtors in the Queen's Bench Prison in 1841. From the sixteenth to the eighteenth century debtors remained the largest group in prison. Debtors were treated differently from criminals and could aspire to a certain degree of comfort. The idea was that of 'coercive imprisonment', with the threat of gaol designed to force debtors to face up to their creditors. In 1790, for example, twelve thousand writs were issued against defaulters in London and Middlesex, but only 10 per cent of the recipients ended up in prison. The Bankruptcy Act of 1861 more or less ended the practice, although imprisonment for debt was not finally abolished until 1970 – and even then with the exception of

debts to the Crown, and non-payment of maintenance orders. The Queen's Bench Prison was located off the Borough High Street in London, and within its walls were two public houses, a coffee-house and numerous shops and stalls. It was demolished in 1880.

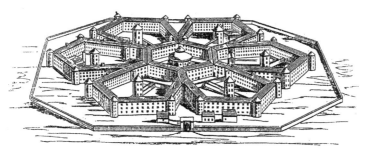

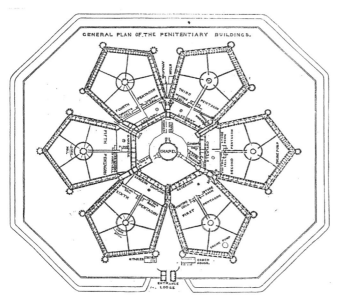

GENERAL PLAN OF THE PENITENTIARY BUILDINGS.

Millbank Penitentiary arose from a failed project to establish a prison based on the ideas of Bentham. After many difficulties, both physical and financial, it was opened in 1816. The historians Sidney and Beatrice Webb described it as 'one of the most costly of all the buildings that the world has seen since the Pyramids in Egypt'. At the centre of the prison was the chapel, around which were arranged six pentagrams distinguished by function and by class of prisoner.

Gloucester prison as were executed. Joseph Kingsmill, chaplain to Pentonville Prison, wrote in 1852 that in the late eighteenth century 'A committal to prison was in fact equivalent, in many cases, to a sentence of death by some frightful disease; and in all, to the utmost extremes of hunger and cold.' Discipline was lax, for gaolers feared to enter parts of many prisons, while the health hazards deterred many would-be reformers from setting foot inside a prison. But not John Howard. Himself a former internee of the French, Howard was High Sheriff of Bedfordshire and visited many county and city prisons as well as prisons in Europe. The problems he described had long been recognised, but his reports caught the public imagination and were in tune with a rising swell of evangelical religion. Howard did not confine himself to the physical needs of the prisoner but was concerned with the moral and spiritual needs as well. As a consequence he raised appreciation of the possibilities of imprisonment as a central part of the penal system and helped to make it a serious competitor to execution or transportation as a punishment.

11

The Reverend Thomas Beames was a passionate advocate of the view that environmental causes lay behind crime and other social problems. In 'The Rookeries of London', published in 1850, he described slum areas of London such as the parish of St Giles, off Charing Cross Road, which he saw as a breeding ground for crime and a school of vice. A spell in prison, it was thought by some reformers, might break the associations made in such places.

VICTORIAN PENAL THEORY: THE SEPARATE AND SILENT SYSTEMS

A number of justifications may be found for imprisonment, and there is no saying that the same ones will prevail at any particular period of time. Imprisonment may be seen as the removal from society, under secure conditions, of those who are considered socially deviant. Its purpose may be seen as a deterrent, the hardships and horrors of prison persuading criminals to mend their ways. Its aim may be the punishment of the offender, possibly beyond the mere loss of freedom that prison inevitably involves. Or it may seek the reformation of the criminal, preparing him (or, less frequently, her) to resume a place as a useful member of the community. When more than one aim is pursued at the same time, there is every possibility that they will conflict with each other.

Penal theory presupposes some knowledge or opinion about what drives people to crime. The answer to that question changed over the course of the nineteenth century, and attitudes to both the provision of prisons and their regime changed accordingly. Much early concern was expressed over the environmental roots of crime, with poor living conditions to blame, especially in the squalor of urban slums. Later, the idea of a 'criminal class' developed, its members genetically disposed to lawbreaking. The reformation of such people was beyond expectation, and rigour became a prevailing quality of prison administration.

'The British Rough' – an engraving by William Small for the 'Graphic', 23rd October 1875. In 1850 the historian and philosopher Thomas Carlyle described criminals in the main as having 'miserable distorted block heads … ape faces, imp faces, angry dog faces, heavy sullen ox faces'. Phrenologists such as George Combe (1788–1858) argued that criminal tendencies in the brain were indicated by the physical shape of the head. For 'criminal types' there was little hope of reformation in prison.

The early-Victorian penal system employed two approaches to the reformation of prisoners, each with a theoretical justification, and a lively debate developed between their proponents. The first was the *separate system*, whereby prisoners were kept in solitary confinement for all or a large part of their sentence. Under the rival *silent system* prisoners, while confined to cells at night, were allowed to associate with each other for work and exercise, although silence was strictly (though ineffectually) enforced.

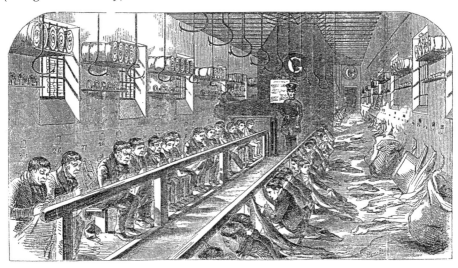

The workshop under the 'silent system' at Millbank Penitentiary. As with workhouses, one of the difficulties with finding work for prison inmates was the importance of not undercutting independent tradespeople outside. A very large part of manufacturing output therefore went to meet the needs of government. The hook-like objects hanging from the ceiling are open gas flares for illumination. (Engraving from Mayhew and Binny)

13

The separate system can be traced back to eighteenth-century reformers, including John Howard, Jonas Hanway and George Onesiphorus Paul, who designed the County Gaol at Gloucester, opened in 1791. The system can be seen as the logical outcome of a growing desire to classify prisoners so that career criminals could not act as mentors in crime to those who were new offenders or had been committed for misdemeanours. Separation was the ultimate classification – each prisoner was unique. That sense of uniqueness appealed to evangelical Christians, who felt that man was naturally inclined to sin, while Quakers had a strong belief in the 'Inner Light'. George Fox, their founder, had written: 'Every man ... is illuminated by the divine light, and I have seen it shine through every man.' But to achieve this a person needed to be quiet, hence the belief in the reforming power of locking criminals up in separate cells. Separation would be all that was enforced on the prisoner. He would not be forced to work; rather he would come to beg for work as a relief from the monotony. Likewise, he would come to welcome the visits of the chaplain, whose encouragement would assist the awakening of conscience.

Penal reformers looked with interest to the United States of America, where, in the 1820s and 1830s, the separate system was pioneered in Philadelphia, while the silent system was developed in Auburn, New York, and later at Sing Sing in the same state.

The Prisons Act of 1835 leant towards the separate system, and it was enthusiastically endorsed by two of the Prison Inspectors whose posts the Act

established, William Crawford and the Reverend Whitworth Russell. However, legislation passed in 1837 prohibited solitary confinement for more than one month, or three months in any one year, and it was not until these limitations were removed in 1839 that a comprehensive change could be contemplated. An immediate result was the construction, between 1840 and 1842, of Pentonville Prison, with 520 separate cells, each 13 feet long by 7 feet wide and 7 feet high (4.0 x 2.1 x 2.1 metres).

Pentonville Prison in London was built in 1840–2 and was intended as a model prison on the separate system. Mayhew and Binny described the 'perfectly Dutch-like cleanliness pervading the place'. Yet critics found much fault with the prison and its regime, arguing, in Robin Evans's words, that it 'was at once too well-appointed to deter, and too dreadful to reform'. Where administrators had more than one aim for prisons such incompatibilities were, perhaps, inevitable. Of the galleries, Mayhew and Binny wrote that the vista was like looking down 'a bunch of Burlington Arcades that had been fitted up in the style of the opera box lobbies with an infinity of little doors'.

A convict at Pentonville Prison (right). At first all wore a brown cloth cap, the peak of which could be turned down to cover the face. The anonymity of prisoners, it was thought, would thus be maintained at times when they associated with one another, for example when at exercise (above). 'The beak', as it was called, was soon abandoned, as it failed in its purpose and merely depressed the men's spirits. (Engravings from Mayhew and Binny)

The debate between advocates of the separate and silent systems took place at many levels. The separatists were criticised for being too optimistic about the improvability of human nature, and it was argued that the repentance apparent in the cell often evaporated when the prisoner once more associated with others. Critics also pointed to the deleterious effects of long periods of solitary confinement, *The Times* describing the separate system in 1842 as 'this maniac-making system'. At a more pragmatic level, while the separate system made it easier to control prisoners, the

A separate cell at Pentonville. Hammocks were a relic of the hulks and survived in some prisons until well into the twentieth century. They were attached to the walls with leather straps, which were liable to break while the convict was asleep. (Engraving from Mayhew and Binny)

The chapels at Pentonville (above) and at Lincoln Prison (left). Prisoners were filed in silence into separate stalls, which screened them from all around – other than the chaplain and the supervising warders. Even so, the convicts still found numerous ways to communicate with each other. (Engraving from Mayhew and Binny)

requirement of separate cells made it difficult to modify existing buildings and required expensive new construction. The advocates of the silent system could equally be accused of over-optimism, for it proved quite impossible to prevent communication between prisoners. Even so, the silence rule, though relaxed in the 1920s, was not formally abolished until the 1950s.

The weight of Home Office opinion fell on the side of the separate system and by 1850 about sixty British prisons had been built or altered to accommodate it. By 1856 two-thirds of English prisons had wholly or partially adopted the system, but enthusiasm eventually waned. The great 'Garrotting Scare' of 1862–3 (in which victims were rendered helpless or unconscious with a garrotte) and a perceived increase in violent crime led to a renewed emphasis on deterrence and punishment, and confidence in the reformatory powers of prison went into decline.

LOCAL PRISONS AND THE DEVELOPMENT OF A NATIONAL SYSTEM

An enormous expansion in the powers of the state occurred in the nineteenth century, and many social and judicial functions previously exercised at a local level came more and more to be controlled by the central government. This was true of the administration of the poor law and of public health – and it also applied to prisons. This raises an important matter of terminology. Not everyone convicted of a crime was termed a 'convict', for that label was restricted to those guilty of felony and confined in a convict prison administered centrally by the national government. For every convict in prison there were many more 'prisoners' languishing in locally administered gaols, often with very short sentences. In many ways the aim of imprisonment differed between the two. The long-term imprisonment or transportation of the convict might lead to his or her reform. The short sentence of a prisoner locked up for a misdemeanour was generally considered insufficient for such a life change, and punishment and deterrence were the only expectations. Between 1837 and 1901 there were more than fifteen million receptions into prisons (including remand prisoners who never returned after their trial). Four out of five sentences handed down were for less than one calendar month.

A first step in the national reform of prisons was made in the 1823 Gaol Act. This required the justices of the peace (who had responsibility for local gaols) to make a systematic inspection of prisons and to file quarterly reports with the Home Secretary. The private trading of gaolers, who tended to run prisons for profit, was abolished, and they were to receive regular payment instead. A move in the direction of decency was that female prisoners were henceforth to be supervised by female warders. Furthermore, gaolers, chaplains and surgeons were to keep work journals. This last provision was typical of a growing

Many towns had more than one prison, being the seat of the County Gaol as well as possessing a town gaol or bridewell, the latter originally being a house of correction where paupers were put to work. Launceston in Cornwall had a County Gaol in the grounds of Launceston Castle (above left), while its town gaol was housed in a room above the South Gate (above right), with a debtors' prison occupying the floor above. A new gaol came into use in nearby Bodmin in 1779, and when it was upgraded to County Gaol in 1829 Launceston Castle prison closed, its buildings being demolished in 1844. Bodmin County Gaol (below) was rebuilt between 1855 and 1858, the 20,000 tons of stone required for its reconstruction being quarried by prisoners. The civil prison closed in 1916, but a naval prison, dating from 1877, occupied part of the site until 1922.

bureaucratisation of public services, and by 1903 it was estimated that there were 450 different Home Office forms relating to prisons.

The 1823 Act made sweeping reforms on paper but reminds us that we should be cautious in our interpretation of the impact of legislation. It had serious flaws. There was no machinery for enforcement, and it was less comprehensive than might be imagined. London debtors' prisons were excluded from its provisions, as were 150 gaols of what were considered, somewhat arbitrarily, to be minor municipalities.

Above and right: *The local prison at Reading was designed by Gilbert Scott and William Moffat, and constructed between 1842 and 1844. A contemporary critic railed against the absurdity of erecting 'a prison at Reading – the handsomest building in Berkshire – on the model of an Elizabethan palace'. However, the regime within was strictly according to the separate system, though the authorities took the unusual step of taking every opportunity to capitalise on the possibilities for moral reflection that solitude offered. Prisoners were taught to write (and required to write essays on theological questions) and to read. 'Read-read-reading Gaol' is what some critics called it, and Lord Brougham remarked in 1849 that it 'might better be called Reading University'. In later years, long after this experiment had been dropped, one of the most famous inmates was Oscar Wilde, who, between 1895 and 1897, served over half of his two-year sentence there.*

Left: *Picking oakum. A reconstruction at Inveraray Prison Museum, Scotland. The old prison was rebuilt in 1816-17, with a new prison added in 1848. The prison closed in 1889. Work undertaken by male prisoners included the making of herring nets and oakum picking. Between 2 and 5 pounds (1–2 kg) of old rope had to be stripped down to its fibres each day. The material was then sold (largely at Greenock) to be used for caulking ships' timbers.*

A step towards tighter enforcement came with the appointment of five Inspectors of Prisons in 1835. They could issue scathing reports to the central government, but still their advice to local prison administrators could not be enforced. Though pressure might be applied, determined local authorities might still hold out against reform.

The execution of John Thurtell in January 1824 outside Hertford County Gaol. Thurtell, who had held a naval commission, was a member of London's gambling set and was found guilty of the murder of William Weare. So great was the publicity given to the case that an estimated fifteen thousand people clogged the town on the morning of the execution. After being cut down, Thurtell's body was sent to the County Hospital and later to St Bartholomew's Hospital, London, for dissection. The scaffold was a temporary structure and so confident were the authorities of the verdict that its construction began even before the commencement of the trial.

In 1844 a Surveyor General of Prisons was appointed, to whom all building plans had to be referred. Penal theory could be implemented through architecture. By 1850 around sixty British prisons had been rebuilt or adapted to conform to the separate system and around eleven thousand separate cells were provided. The preferred design for prisons was the radial pattern, whereby a number of wings were arranged around a central building. An increase in the number of prisoners (or separate categories of prisoner) could be allowed for by adding new wings to the existing cores, while more radical expansion could be accomplished by the addition of new hubs. Between 1842 and 1877 nineteen radial prisons were constructed in England, ranging in size from those with between two hundred and four hundred cells to large, urban prisons that could accommodate up to one thousand prisoners.

In 1877 local prisons came fully under government control through a consolidating Prisons Act. The Home Secretary became responsible for all prisons, and a Prison Commission of up to five members was appointed to administer the law, although the appointment of senior prison officers remained the duty of the Home Secretary.

An immediate effect of the 1877 Prisons Act was to accelerate the closure of local prisons. Between 1862 and 1877 eighty of the 193 local prisons had been shut down, and by 1895 the number had fallen to fifty-six.

The Governor's house of the North Tipperary County Gaol, Nenagh, built in 1840–2. The prison closed in 1886 and, after use as a convent and a girls' secondary school, eventually became the Nenagh Heritage and Family Research Centre. Irish convict prisons (as opposed to local prisons) came under a separate Convict Prisons Board in 1854. At a time when the belief in the ability to reform prisoners went into decline in England, it lingered on in Ireland, where a marks system attempted to encourage prisoners to cooperate in order to earn privileges.

CONVICT PRISONS AND PENAL SERVITUDE

It was in the nineteenth century that the first prisons to be built and administered by the central government came into being, although there were abortive plans to build a national penitentiary as early as the 1770s. It was not until 1821 that the national penitentiary at Millbank was completed, the prison acting as a holding point for those under sentence of transportation. Pentonville followed in 1842 and was intended as a model prison, both architecturally and in the nature of its strict, separate regime. Here, prisoners served a probationary period in solitary confinement before transfer to a public-works prison and subsequent transportation. Three public-works prisons (Portland, Portsmouth and Chatham) were built between 1848 and 1856, and their number was expanded after the abolition of transportation.

Public-works prisons were lauded as a means whereby criminals could repay their debt to society, for work of significant public importance was carried out, including the construction of sea defences at Portland, dockyard building at Chatham and land reclamation on Dartmoor. The labour was severe. For example, the 'Report on Discipline and Management of the Convict Prisons' issued in 1854 recorded that 'a party of from ten, twelve to fourteen on average drag a loaded cart, the weight of which is from one and a half to two and a quarter tons, a distance of from ten to sixteen miles backwards and forwards

A working party leaves Dartmoor prison at the start of the twentieth century. One of the original motives for siting the prison at Princetown was that the moor might be reclaimed, and prison farming at Dartmoor lasted for nearly two hundred years. Eventually some 1600 acres (650 hectares) were cultivated, but most of the stock and equipment were auctioned off in August 2004, since when only small-scale farming on 28 acres (11 hectares) has been practised. The prison farm was not as idyllic as it sounds, for Dartmoor possesses some of the bleakest landscape in Britain.

A

Order of Licence under the Penal Servitude Acts, 1853 to 1891.

WHITEHALL,

day of 190

HIS MAJESTY is graciously pleased to

grant to
who was convicted of

at the
for the
on the day of 18 , and was
then and there sentenced to be kept in Penal Servitude for the term of

and is now confined in the Prison.

His Royal Licence to be at large from the day of his liberation under this order, during the remaining portion of his said term of Penal Servitude, unless the said

shall before the expiration of the said term, be convicted on indictment of some offence within the United Kingdom, in which case such Licence will be immediately forfeited by law, or unless it shall please His Majesty sooner to revoke or alter such Licence

This Licence is given subject to the conditions endorsed upon the same, upon the breach of any of which it will be liable to be revoked, whether such breach is followed by a conviction or not.

And His Majesty hereby orders that the said
be set at liberty within Thirty Days
from the date of this Order

Given under my Hand and Seal,

Signed,

TRUE COPY. }
Licence to be at Large. }

Director of Convict Prisons.

W B & L (480)—39629—1000-3-01

The modern parole system has its origins in the 'ticket-of-leave' or licence, under which penal servitude prisoners were enabled, while supervised and under licence, to complete their sentences outside prison. The practice of licensing prisoners originated in Australia and was introduced into Britain by the Penal Servitude Act of 1853. By the early 1860s over two thousand prisoners were being released under licence from convict prisons each year. The prospect of eventually earning a licence acted as an incentive to good behaviour. Even so, tickets-of-leave were a matter of controversy between those who feared criminals being allowed into the community and those who argued that the supervision involved made it difficult to find honest work.

during the day'. The time that a prisoner spent in a public-works prison varied according to the length of his sentence and his conduct, for good behaviour was rewarded by early embarkation to Australia, where he might immediately be released on licence.

Following the refusal of Van Diemen's Land to accept any

In public-works prisons, where convicts worked outside the prison, security was an important issue. In 1850 the task was given to the military, who were replaced in 1854 by a body of armed pensioners. This 'Dad's Army' proved inefficient, and in 1857 a regular body of younger men was formed into a civil guard. The uniform was described as 'a sort of cross between that of a policeman and a soldier. The men were armed with a loaded rifle at full cock.' The civil guard, which was never employed in local prisons, was abolished around 1919.

Convicts manhandling a cart at the beginning of the twentieth century.

more convicts, a new sentence of penal servitude was introduced (which lingered on until 1948) by the Penal Servitude Act of 1853. Those sentenced to less than fourteen years of transportation were to face penal servitude in a British convict prison. As transportation to Western Australia ceased in 1867, penal servitude became the sole long-term punishment. As such, incentives to good behaviour had to be built in, and a progressive system of rewards and punishments was developed, relating to severity of labour, earnings, the receiving and sending of letters, visits and diet. A sentence of penal servitude could not be given for less than three years, but a shorter sentence could be made more severe by the imposition of hard labour (up to a maximum of two years). Many prisoners preferred three or four years of penal servitude to two years of hard labour. Prisoners sentenced to the latter spent their first two weeks on a plank bed (and continued to do so until 1945) and also had an inferior diet and heavier labour.

Although many transportees hoped to return to Britain, few actually did, and the pain of parting from loved ones must have been immense. There was a natural desire to leave some tangible memento, but what could a poor man give? The answer is that many gave love tokens, often engraved with their own hands or the hands of a more skilled convict. One of the favourite mediums was the 'cartwheel penny', some 36 mm in diameter. Defacing the coin (a criminal act in itself) seems also to have been a symbolic deed aimed at the state power that had condemned them. One of those shown here (left-hand side, second down) was engraved for J. Fletcher and has the following lines on the reverse: 'tho time may pass & years may fly & every hope decay & die & every joyfull dream be set but thee I never can forget.' It dates from the early 1830s. That of Thomas Alsop (right-hand side, second from bottom) reads: 'Accept this dear Mother from your Unfortunate son – Thos. Alsop – Transported July 25 Aged 21 1833.' Alsop was transported for life for stealing a sheep. He died in Australia in 1891.

The exercise yard at Newgate, from Gustave Doré and Blanchard Jerrold, 'London: A Pilgrimage', published in 1872. The French illustrator Gustave Doré (1832–83) was gifted in capturing the essential spirit of a scene, which appealed to him more than strict historical accuracy. Van Gogh was greatly taken with this engraving, of which he painted a version of his own.

LIFE IN PRISON

For the first-time prisoner one of the biggest shocks must have been the admission procedure, for his new status was apparent from the very moment that the prison gates closed behind him. Prison staff made a physical examination in order to provide a description for their records, noting any 'distinguishing marks'. For much of the nineteenth century there was great difficulty in establishing the identity of prisoners, especially re-offenders who might use an alias. Incoming prisoners were often lined up in the exercise yard for an identity parade, at which special 'recognising officers' attempted to spot old offenders. A Select Committee of the House of Lords in 1863 advocated the photographing of all prisoners, a practice with which some prisons had already experimented, and which became general after the Prevention of Crime Act, 1871. Fingerprinting had been introduced by the end of the century.

Prisoners were required to hand over all personal property and were subjected to a compulsory bath. No one escaped this humiliating ritual, although conditions varied from prison to prison. An ex-prisoner described the baths at Newgate in 1877 as clean, and up to the standard of second-class public baths in London. In 1880, on the other hand, a former inmate of Kirkdale Gaol at Liverpool described the bath water as 'not unlike mutton broth'. Getting the

24

prisoner clean was not the sole function of the bath. Of greater importance, perhaps, was its function as a rite of passage. The prisoner's old identity was erased and replaced by the anonymity of prison life. This transition was emphasised by the haircut, the issue of a uniform and the receiving of a prison number by which he would now be known. The hair of the convict was cropped to the scalp. Not until three months before the end of his sentence was he allowed to grow it again. Prisoners were also read the prison rules. In 1911 there were 313

An exercise yard at Holloway Prison at the end of the nineteenth century. Most of the men appear to be remand prisoners, who were allowed to wear their own clothing before trial.

Above: *Letter-writing in Wandsworth Gaol. The original caption to this photograph, from a book published c.1896, read: 'It is a humane regulation which permits the prisoners in all our gaols to communicate by letter with their friends and relatives at certain fixed intervals, and under certain conditions. It need hardly be said that these conditions include the right of the prison authorities to peruse every letter before it leaves the gaol, and to stop any message which they think likely to prove detrimental to discipline, or which is in any way undesirable.' In reality, arrangements for letter-writing could be far from humane. The opportunity to send and receive letters was always regarded as a privilege rather than a right and could be taken away more or less at the whim of an officer.*

Convict dress varied according to the category of the prisoner, and there were at least ten variations. Men of good character could secure a blue uniform, while those who struck officers or ran away were obliged to wear particoloured uniforms. The broad arrow (a mark of government property) even extended to the pattern of nails on the soles of their boots.

26

published rules in local prisons, but in addition there were 1441 unpublished Standing Orders that regulated the minutiae of prison life.

In local prisons convict dress was varied, although there was greater uniformity within the convict prisons. Even so, prisoners serving a sentence of penal servitude had uniforms in a variety of colour combinations or markings that denoted their status within the convict hierarchy. Little attention was paid to size, and until late in the nineteenth century underwear was not issued. The men were supplied with boots – often old, repaired ones – which in public-works prisons could weigh as much as 14 pounds (6 kg). The Irish patriot Jeremiah O'Donovan Rossa, who was sentenced to penal servitude for life (he served eight years before exile to America), wrote of his boots: 'I put them on and the weight of them seemed to fasten me to the ground.'

Prison authorities tried to keep prisoners isolated from each other, either by separate confinement or by strict application of the silence rule. It was a forlorn hope. Prisoners, whether confined to their cells or mixing in associated labour or exercise, found numerous ways of communicating with each other. Messages could be tapped out on walls or water-pipes, while the chapel offered special opportunities. Writing in 1898, Frederick Brocklehurst, a former convict, explained how a prisoner wishing to converse with a neighbour would emphasise the first word of each line of a hymn and then drop into a lower tone. He gave the example of the hymn 'Nearer my God to Thee':

(cresc.) 'Nearer'	(dim.) 'How are you Jack?'
(cresc.) 'Nearer'	(dim.) 'All right.'
(cresc.) 'E'en'	(dim.) 'When are you going out?'
(cresc.) 'That'	(dim.) 'Monday week' (etc., etc.)

He explained that the longer the line of the hymn, the greater chance there was of squeezing in a long sentence in place of the one meant to be sung. Even the treadwheel could be used to mask conversation, the trick being to speak in a pitch other than that of the wheel. Nor did communication have to be verbal. Sign language played its part. To indicate to a fellow inmate that tobacco was desired, the prisoner touched his nose. 'Snout' has been the prison slang for tobacco ever since.

Prison food was plain and monotonous. At Pentonville and most other prisons the diet consisted of three-quarters of a pint of cocoa for breakfast, made from flaked cocoa and milk and sweetened with molasses. Dinner was four ounces of meat, half a pint of soup and a pound of potatoes. For supper the prisoner received a pint of gruel sweetened with molasses, together with one and a quarter pounds of bread, and salt. At public-works prisons, where labour was heavy, the diet was more ample and more varied, and, as they progressed to higher stages, penal-servitude prisoners received further nutritional rewards. Regulations introduced in 1899 improved dietaries somewhat, although complex categories remained. Writing in 1903, George Griffith observed that 'The dietary, in ordinary, consists of coarse brown bread, boiled meat, potatoes, gruel and cocoa. A man must either be sick or in the highest possible class and character to get tea instead of cocoa and have his meat roasted instead of boiled.'

Griffith draws attention to the power of the prison doctor to increase or alter diet, and these powers were considerable, extending to absolute discretion with regard to the severity of punishment, and the authority to order rest in the prison hospital. Old lags became skilled at manipulating the sick parade, an example of

Treadwheels were used by medieval builders and a fourteenth-century example survives within the spire of Salisbury Cathedral. Their use in prisons was specifically sanctioned by the Penitentiary Act of 1779, but it was not until the design was modified by William Cubitt that they became widespread. Cubitt developed a new type of treadwheel while employed as chief engineer for Ransomes of Ipswich, a firm of agricultural engineers. Unlike earlier examples, it was operated from the exterior of the wheel rather than from within. Cubitt installed such a wheel at Brixton Prison in 1821 (above). It was used for grinding corn, but many advocates of the treadwheel favoured its punitive rather than its productive potential. By 1824 there were seventy-five wheels in forty-nine prisons spread across twenty-six counties.

Various types of brake and governor were designed to make the operation of the wheel more arduous. At Coldbath Fields (below) a fan-like structure was erected on the roof to act as an

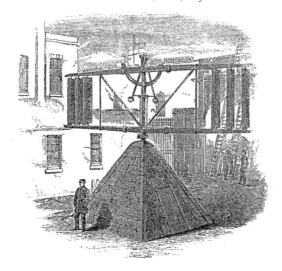

adjustable air-brake, leading prisoners to say that they were 'grinding the wind'. The action of working the treadwheel was likened to climbing. As the wheel fell away beneath his feet, the prisoner had to lift his body to the next step. In the 1850s the Prison Discipline Society advocated a daily stint equivalent to an ascent of 12,000 feet (3658 metres), while at Stafford 16,630 feet (5069 metres) (well over half the height of Mount Everest) was the daily norm. Such physical effort could be greatly deleterious to health, but old hands learned techniques for minimising exhaustion. The engraving from the 'Illustrated London News' of 4th July 1874 (right) suggests that the prisoner on the left is more overcome by the heat and tiredness than his two resting colleagues. Generally prisoners worked for fifteen minutes on the wheel and then rested for five. The late-nineteenth-century photo-graph from Portsmouth Prison (below) shows stilt-like posts that were used for stepping on and off the wheel.

In 1899 the use of treadwheels for non-productive purposes was abolished, and two years later (when there were thirteen left) their use was prohibited entirely. The sole surviving treadwheel may be seen at Beaumaris Prison Museum.

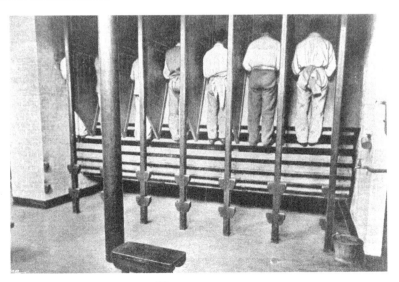

the many ways in which prison discipline bore less heavily on repeat offenders than upon first-timers.

It is difficult to imagine anything better fashioned to depress the spirit than the Victorian prison cell. In most local prisons the cells measured 13 by 7 feet (4 by 2 metres), with a height of 9 feet (3 metres). In convict prisons (where inmates spent less time in their cells) the dimensions were somewhat less, one former prisoner describing his cell as smaller than a third-class railway carriage compartment. The outer wall was generally plastered so that attempts to break out were more easily detected. The tiny-paned window was so high up that it was necessary to stand on the stool in order to look out – and that was a punishable offence. Cells were often stuffy in summer, cold in winter, and poorly lit. When town gas was introduced many prisons fitted gas jets in cells, but the danger of suicide by self-asphyxiation or hanging from the jet eventually led to their being replaced by thick, fixed glass windows framing gas burners ignited from outside.

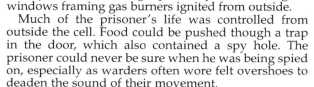

Much of the prisoner's life was controlled from outside the cell. Food could be pushed though a trap in the door, which also contained a spy hole. The prisoner could never be sure when he was being spied on, especially as warders often wore felt overshoes to deaden the sound of their movement.

A crank at Inveraray Gaol (left). Many penologists preferred the use of the hand crank to that of the treadwheel, for it fitted better with the separate system of imprisonment and offered less likelihood of injury from slipping or falling. Individual effort could be accurately measured, and in some prisons a tariff of turns was laid down which had to be completed before the prisoner received the next meal. The engraving (below) shows a prisoner at crank labour at Wandsworth Prison in London in the early 1860s. At Coldbath Fields (also in London) the cranks were linked to the treadwheel, but in such a way that they each worked against the other. A French commentator, M. C. Moreau-Christophe, wrote: 'I know of nothing harder or more degrading than this work.'

A cell at Portland Convict Prison in the late nineteenth century. Cells in convict prisons were generally occupied only at night, hence the cheap corrugated-iron partitions. Convicts were required to polish their zinc eating utensils (always referred to as 'tinware') to a military shine. Some prisoners preferred not to use them in order to preserve the shine. A warder bearing a grudge could make a prisoner's life more difficult by sprinkling salt on to the zinc, which soon pitted it, leaving black marks that required much effort to remove.

Chief among the furniture of the cell was the bed. Except where hammocks lingered as a relic of the hulks, plank beds were the norm; and for prisoners sentenced to less than one month, and for those in the first month of a longer sentence, there was no mattress. The 1865 Prison Act brought in the hard plank bed, part of an increasingly severe regime introduced in the 1860s and 1870s, when punishment and deterrence came to take precedence over reformation. Its use continued until 1945. Sleep evaded many, but it is difficult to say how the majority of prisoners fared. For some, adjustment must have been painful, but for others prison conditions would have been comparable (perhaps even preferable) to those endured outside.

The experience of prison depended very much on the individual and his or her background, and it is worth remembering that ex-prisoners who published accounts of their imprisonment were not a representative sample. Their accounts of the arduousness of prison labour have to be treated with equal caution. Prison labour highlights the dilemmas faced by authorities pursuing different penal ends. Was labour meant to encourage prisoners to find fulfilment in honest work, so that they might lead productive lives on release? Or was labour part of the punishment, with unproductive work designed to deny prisoners the satisfaction of seeing a result for their effort? The treadwheel and the crank typified the latter approach, as did 'shot drill', where men walked the equivalent of 1³/4 miles (3 km) daily, picking up and putting down, at every three paces, cannon balls weighing 24 pounds (11 kg). 'It is impossible', wrote Henry Mayhew, 'to imagine anything more *ingeniously useless.*'

Productive work presented the problem of undercutting free labourers outside, with the result that prison work concentrated on government contracts. At the end of the nineteenth century, prisoners at Parkhurst made hammocks, fenders and nets for the Navy, and coir beds for the Army. Dartmoor prisoners kept the Navy supplied with chain-bound coaling baskets, while 720 pounds (327 kg) of Post Office string were produced each week by women prisoners in the Aylesbury Prison twine shop. Dartmoor prisoners made all the boots for the Metropolitan Police, for whom a more bizarre service was provided by convicts at Chatham: they were given the task of smashing up with hammers the old enamel hackney-carriage licence plates to prevent their illicit use.

PRISON OFFICERS

It is easy to see prisoners as powerless and prison warders as all-powerful, but this would be far from the truth. The reality of prison life is not to be revealed by rule books and administrative structures alone. Prison officers were subject to draconian regulations. Writing in 1852, Joseph Kingsmill, Chaplain of Pentonville Prison, quoted from the 'admirable regulations' laid down for warders in the convict prisons:

> Intoxication will be visited with dismissal; and it will not be taken into consideration at what place the act of intemperance was committed, nor whether the officer was or was not thereby considered incapable of performing his duty... Swearing and improper language; knowingly incurring debts which they are unable to pay; the habit of frequenting public houses; keeping bad company; gambling or card-playing, will be considered a sufficient reason for the dismissal of an officer.

Officers were forbidden to talk to prisoners and were even prohibited from conversing with each other while on duty. Prison was a closed society, and there is a real sense that officers were themselves prisoners both inside and outside the walls, for much of their off-duty life was also supervised, including their housing.

Many warders were used to harsh discipline, having come from a military

background. In 1893, for example, 66 per cent of applications for subordinate posts in local prisons came from men with a background in the Army or Navy, and a roughly similar percentage of those actually appointed were of the same origin. The prison service operated within a paramilitary structure. Officers wore a uniform, paraded for duty, were subject to

Above: *An improving tract issued by the Religious Tract Society in the late 1830s. The chaplain visits two prisoners, one of whom predictably repents of his capital crime and is given an eleventh-hour reprieve (his sentence being commuted to transportation for life). His obdurate companion, on the other hand, goes to the gallows. Tracts such as these were often used by prison chaplains with an enthusiastic faith in their transforming powers.*

Right: *A prison officer and two juvenile offenders at Parkhurst Prison on the Isle of Wight. The prison officers wore blue frock-coats, cloth caps and a leather belt and straps holding keys. Changes to Army uniforms were reflected in those of prison officers, who later wore a shorter jacket, with a shako replacing the flat, peaked cap. The engraving is from the 'Illustrated London News' of 13th March 1847.*

'In Trouble' was the title of this early-twentieth-century book illustration. The military bearing of the prison warder is impressive. Hardly less striking, however, is the depiction of the convict, whose fine features and straight back are a far cry from the popular image of the criminal.

quasi-military discipline and were even armed according to rank – warders in convict prisons were armed with a bayonet, while the principal warder carried a cutlass. Prison governors came from the officer class and bore the stamp of gentlemen. In 1850 George Jacob Holyoake wrote of Captain Mason, governor of Gloucester Prison: 'As blandly and courteously as he wished me good morning, he would have conducted me to the gallows, had instruction to that effect reached him. He would have apologised for the inconvenience, but would have hung me while I was saying "Pray don't mention it".'

Yet, for all this, prison staff knew that they were living on a volcano, and a symbiotic relationship developed with prisoners, for each could make the life of the other either easier or more difficult. A former convict, 'A Ticket-of-leave Man', wrote in 1879 that 'There is a tacit understanding between all "second-timers" and old thieves, and the officers who have charge of them. If the officer is caught in any dereliction of duty he is liable to a fine; these old thieves act as his spies, and take care that he is *not* caught. In return he allows the thieves to fetch what they call an easy lagging.'

Prison warders were poorly paid, with the almost inevitable consequence that there was great temptation to corruption. 'A Ticket-of-leave Man' referred to the 'underground railway' that he had encountered, whereby convicts got friends outside the prison to pay warders to bring in contraband articles, which in his case included food and newspapers.

The wardresses' recreation room at Holloway Prison at the start of the twentieth century. 'The female officers', ran the accompanying text in 'Living London', 'have a life full of anxieties, even dangers, for assaults are not uncommon; yet are they mild mannered, forbearing to their troublesome sisterhood, and have strong claims to the respect and esteem of the public at large.'

WOMEN AND CHILDREN IN PRISON

In the second half of the nineteenth century, 20 per cent of those convicted of crime were women, and they constituted 17 per cent of the prison population. The corresponding figures for the late twentieth century were 12^1/$_2$ per cent and under 4 per cent respectively. In other words, women constituted a significantly larger proportion of the prison population than they do in modern times.

In late-Victorian England well over 90 per cent of female prisoners were given short custodial sentences and were therefore confined to local prisons, where they made up around a quarter of the inmates. So far was the prison from being 'less eligible' than the conditions of many poor women that a short prison sentence was deliberately sought by some, who saw it as better than the workhouse. Mary Gordon, the first Lady Inspector of Prisons, reported a woman who claimed that, compared with a stay in the workhouse, 'Here I can have a room to myself, and what with three meals a day, and the doctor whenever I want him, I'm better off here.' Women prisoners referred to a sentence of a few days as 'a wash and brush up'.

The Victorians had an idealised view of womanhood, which (in many respects) was shared by working-class women as well as the middle class from whom the ideal sprang. The 'fallen woman' is a stock character in Victorian literature, and although Christians believed that all people – men and women alike – had, since Adam, fallen into sin, the sins of Eve somehow seemed less 'natural'. Men's crimes were seen as a perversion of their nature, leading to an antisocial expression of their inherent qualities of risk-taking, courage and physical vigour. But women who committed crimes betrayed their very nature. In 1866 the writer of an article in the *Cornhill Magazine* (in a manner revealing racial as well as gender stereotyping) stated: 'Criminal women, as a class, are found to be more uncivilized than the savage, more degraded than the slave, less true to all natural and womanly instincts than the untutored squaw of a North American Indian tribe.'

In the course of time this view of female criminality as being unnatural led to pathological explanations. More than mere moral failure was the cause; criminal women were psychologically disordered and were to be treated in a manner not unlike that of the

The strains of imprisonment made women prisoners prone to self-harm, and to what was generally known as 'breaking out', or exhibiting riotous behaviour, 'amounting almost to a frenzy, smashing their windows, tearing up their clothes, destroying every useful article within their reach, generally yelling, shouting or singing as if they were maniacs' (Report of the Directors of Convict Prisons, Millbank, 1853). Violent women who destroyed their clothes were restrained by a canvas dress not dissimilar to a strait-jacket.

Making sacks in Holloway Prison at the turn of the twentieth century. Plank beds were taken down during the day and rested against a wall of the cell, with the mattress rolled up in a corner.

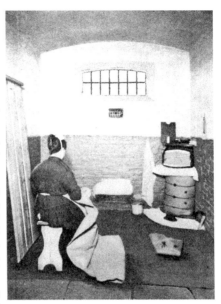

treatment of lunatics. At the end of the nineteenth century, when there was a great debate about 'national deterioration' – a debate that embraced eugenics as a means of preserving the national 'stock' – criminal women came to be dealt with more firmly. In 1898 the Inebriates Act allowed for the preventative detention, for up to three years, of habitual drunkards and those who had committed serious offences while under the influence of drink. Between 1898 and 1914 women made up 80 per cent of admissions to inebriate reformatories, but the movement had little impact. By the time they had reached this stage women were beyond moral influence or had indeed become seriously impaired mentally.

In the early Victorian period, when there were such high hopes of the reforming power of the silent and separate systems, there was particular optimism that female prisoners might be restored to their 'natural' feminine state. It was argued that, because women were used to the confinement of the home, separate confinement in prison offered particular opportunities for reformation. There was a greater flexibility in the prison regime, and women prisoners were treated far more as individuals. Female warders were thought to possess a greater moral influence than their male colleagues, and their conduct was expected to be exemplary. The expectation was too high, and recourse was had to Lady Visitors – middle-class women who, it was hoped, would rekindle the spark of appropriate feminine behaviour. The

Summer dress of star-class prisoners at Aylesbury women's prison. On entry to prison, women (like men) were obliged to have their hair cut. They were also subject to uniform regulations. However, attempts made by prisoners to improve their physical appearance were generally approved of as a sign of returning femininity. The Visiting Committee at Aylesbury prison reported in 1907 that women should be encouraged 'to do their hair in any becoming and neat way they please'.

35

influence of respectable women might turn the prisoner back to the path of respectability. An anonymous author, writing in 1864, argued that 'A woman on entering a convict prison should feel that however vicious her past life has been, she is come to a place where she has a character to regain and support.' And 'a character' *was* important if a woman were to find employment, for without at least a veneer of respectability women could not compete in the market for domestic service or shop work. It is hard to tell what impact all this had, but, since most women received short prison sentences, the effect would have been minimised.

For much of the period the female prison population appears to have been more homogeneous than the male. Observers remarked that there were few educated women in prison, partly, no doubt, because they were denied most of the opportunities to commit 'white collar' crime. The situation changed with the development of the women's suffrage movement. Imprisoned suffragettes were self-confident, less deferential and better able to publicise the plight of women prisoners. On balance, their condition seems to have been not so different from that of the men. Stephen Hobhouse and Fenner Brockway put it concisely: 'In both [men's and women's prisons] there are the small, nameless humiliations, the inevitable abuses, or a too-absolute power, and the infringement of rules to the prisoner's disadvantage.'

The boys' schoolroom at Tothill Fields Prison, London. Schooling presented the prison authorities with a dilemma. On the one hand the provision of education might help to break the cycle of deprivation and crime. On the other, it provided young offenders with a service that could be ill-afforded by many independent labourers. At Parkhurst Prison (originally an institution for juvenile offenders) the educational programme was so concentrated that many boys hoped for clerical work on release. However, in 1849 (in the belief that, however academically qualified, the boys would not get such jobs) the authorities scaled down academic teaching and gave greater emphasis to industrial training.

Boys exercising at Tothill Fields Prison in the early 1860s.

One last group of people to be found in prisons needs to be considered, namely children. There were two ways in which a child might experience the inside of a prison. Some were born there or were admitted on the commital of a nursing mother. At the age of twelve months babies were meant to be removed to the care of relatives or else admitted into the workhouse. In practice the period was sometimes extended beyond a year, and Hobhouse and Brockway wrote of a three-year-old boy whose mother and grandmother were both in the same prison, 'who ran all about the place and stopping at a cell door would knock and call, "You all right, granny?"' Though the psychological impact of incarceration on a toddler cannot have been good, the benefits were said to extend beyond the mother, for the presence of a child brought a breath of life to many troubled women in prison.

Other children were in prison because the courts had sent them there – for example little Sarah Ann Franks, aged eight, who was sentenced in 1857 to three months in Taunton County Gaol for the theft of peppermints. And she was by no means the youngest to receive a prison sentence or sentence of transportation. Many wrote of the deleterious effect of prison on children and youths. The Reverend Joseph Kingsmill wrote in 1852 that 'the young are taught the vices of their elders, and many who enter the prison naughty boys, it is to be feared, leave it accomplished thieves'.

Much of the credit for reforming the treatment of children must go to Mary Carpenter, a Bristol philanthropist. She took street children into a privately run

Borstal boys learning building trade skills c.1910. The Borstal system was meant to deal with those aged between sixteen and twenty-one, when, it was argued, 'a boy's wages no longer satisfy and a man's wages cannot be claimed, when the strong boy feels restless and the weak boy hopeless'. After five months of good behaviour boys were promoted to 'blue dress' and trusted to work outside the institution, sometimes alone.

reformatory school and gave evidence on juvenile offenders to a House of Lords Committee set up in 1853. As a result the Youthful Offenders Act was passed in the following year, allowing courts to sentence children to between two and five years in a reformatory school. By 1857 forty-five such schools had been established, many by private individuals supported by local authorities (though inspected by the Prison Inspectorate). In 1860 control passed to the Home Office.

Not until the Children Act of 1908 was imprisonment for children under the age of fourteen abolished, with restrictions placed on that of young persons between the ages of fourteen and sixteen. The Prevention of Crime Act of the same year extended nationally the Borstal experiment that had been established for youths of sixteen to twenty-one in a largely empty convict prison at Borstal in Kent. The regime consisted of education, physical training and trade training. The 'lads', as they were called, were taught to play football and cricket, for 'a knowledge of them is a passport to decent company on their release'. This was written in 1910, the year in which Edward VII died. The system was still far from perfect (what penal system ever is?) but prisons had come a long way since early Victorian times.

FURTHER READING

Brodie, Allan, *et al. Behind Bars. The Hidden Architecture of England's Prisons*. English Heritage, 1999.
Brodie, Allan, *et al. English Prisons: An Architectural History*. English Heritage, 2002.
Evans, Robin. *The Fabrication of Virtue: English Prison Architecture 1750–1840*. Cambridge University Press, 1982.
Forsythe, William James. *The Reform of Prisoners 1830–1900*. Croom Helm, 1987.
Griffith, George. *Sidelights on Convict Life*. John Lang, 1903.
Harding, Christopher, *et al. Imprisonment in England and Wales: A Concise History*. Croom Helm, 1985.
Hawkings, David T. *Criminal Ancestors*. Alan Sutton, 1996.
Higgs, Michelle. *Prison Life in Victorian England*. Tempus, 2007.
Hobhouse, Stephen, and Brockway, A. Fenner. *English Prisons Today*. Longman, Green, 1922.
Ignatieff, Michael. *A Just Measure of Pain*. Penguin, 1989.
Kingsmill, Joseph. *Chapters on Prisons and Prisoners*. Longman, Green, Brown and Longman, 1852.
Mayhew, Henry, and Binny, John. *The Criminal Prisons of London*. Griffin, 1862.
Priestley, Philip. *Victorian Prison Lives*. Pimlico, 1999. Contains an excellent list of prison memoirs and biographies.
Thomas, J. E. *The English Prison Officer Since 1850*. Routledge & Kegan Paul, 1972.
'A Ticket-of-Leave Man'. *Convict Life, or Revelations Concerning Convicts and Convict Prisons*. Wyman, 1879.
Wilkinson, Robert. *The Law of Prisons*. Knight & Co, 1878.
Zedner, Lucia. *Women, Crime and Custody in Victorian England*. Clarendon Press, 1991.

USEFUL WEBSITES

Her Majesty's Prison Service: www.hmprisonservice.gov.uk
Rossbret Institutions: www.institutions.org.uk/prisons – a nationwide site with much historical information on prisons.
University College London Bentham Project: www.ucl.ac.uk/Bentham-Project
Victorian London: www.victorianlondon.org – a fascinating site operated by Lee Jackson, with a section on London prisons.

The staff at HM Convict Prison, Portland, in 1906. Many of the warders wear service medals, indicating their military or naval background, while senior uniformed staff are distinguished by their swords. The governor and his assistants (including the chaplains) wear civilian dress, indicating that these are 'gentlemen'. One question remains – who is minding the shop?

PLACES TO VISIT

Visitors are advised to check the times and dates of opening before travelling.

Anne of Cleves House, 52 Southover High Street, Lewes, East Sussex BN7 1JA. Telephone: 01273 474610. Website: www.sussexpast.co.uk The museum has displays relating to Lewes Prison.

Beaumaris Gaol, Steeple Lane, Beaumaris, Anglesey LL58 8EP. Telephone: 01248 810921. Website: www.anglesey.gov.uk/english/culture/gaol.htm

Bodmin Jail, Berrycombe Road, Bodmin, Cornwall PL31 2NR. Telephone: 01208 76292. Website: www.bodminjail.org

Cambridge and County Folk Museum, 2–3 Castle Street, Cambridge CB3 0AQ. Telephone: 01223 355159. Website: www.folkmuseum.org.uk

Clerkenwell House of Detention, Clerkenwell, London EC1R 0AS. Telephone: 020 7253 9494.

Dartmoor Prison Heritage Centre, HMP Dartmoor, Princetown, Devon PL20 6RR. Telephone: 01822 892130. Website: www.dartmoor-prison.co.uk

Guildhall Museum, High Street, Rochester, Kent ME1 1PY. Telephone: 01634 848717. Website: www.medway.gov.uk/index/leisure/museums The museum features a two-tier gallery recreating a prison hulk.

Inveraray Gaol, Inveraray, Argyll, Scotland PA32 8TX. Telephone: 01499 302381. Website: www.inverarayjail.co.uk

The Judges' Lodging, Broad Street, Presteigne, Powys LD8 2AD. Telephone: 01544 260650. Website: www.judgeslodging.org.uk

Kilmainham Gaol, Inchicore Road, Kilmainham, Dublin 8, Republic of Ireland. Telephone: 00353 1453 5984. Website: www.visitdublin.com

Lincoln Castle (and Prison), Castle Hill, Lincoln LN1 3AA. Telephone: 01522 511068. Websites: www.lincolncastle.com and www.lincolnshire.gov.uk

Museum of London, London Wall, London EC2Y 5HN. Telephone: 0870 444 3852. Website: www.museumoflondon.org.uk

The NCCL Galleries of Justice, Shire Hall, High Pavement, Lace Market, Nottingham NG1 1HN. Telephone: 0115 952 0555. Website: www.galleriesofjustice.org.uk

The Old Gaol Museum, Market Hill, Buckingham MK18 1JX. Telephone: 01280 823020. Website: www.mkheritage.co.uk/ogb

Oxford Prison. Oxford Castle served as the county gaol until 1966. The prison, a Grade I listed building, has been converted into a luxury hotel, preserving many of its historic features. For information contact Malmaison Oxford Hotel, 3 Oxford Castle, Oxford OX1 1AY (telephone for reservations: 0845 365 4247; email oxford@malmaison.com; website: www.malmaison.com/oxford.asp). Also in the castle there is a museum and heritage centre, called Unlocked. For information contact Oxford Preservation Trust (telephone: 01865 242918; website: www.oxfordpreservation.org.uk)

Peterborough Museum and Art Gallery, Priestgate, Peterborough PE1 1LF. Telephone: 01733 343329. Website: www.peterboroughheritage.org.uk The museum has the largest collection of memorabilia relating to the camp for French prisoners of war at Norman Cross.

Powysland Museum, The Canal Wharf, Welshpool, Powys SY21 7AQ. Telephone: 01938 554656. Website: www.powys.gov.uk

Ripon Prison and Police Museum, 27 St Marygate, Ripon, North Yorkshire HG4 1LX. Website: www.riponmuseums.co.uk

Ruthin Gaol, Clwyd St, Ruthin, Denbighshire LL15 1HP. Telephone: 01824 708281. Website: www.ruthingaol.co.uk

HM Tower of London, London, EC3N 4AB. Telephone: 0870 756 6060 (infoline). Website: www.hrp.org.uk

Wymondham Heritage Museum, 10 The Bridewell, Norwich Road, Wymondham NR18 0NS. Telephone: 01953 600205 or 01953 607494. Website: www.wymondham-norfolk.co.uk/heritage/museum.htm The Heritage Centre is housed in a former bridewell, used as Norfolk County Women's Prison between 1831 and 1878.

York Castle Museum, Eye of York, York YO1 9RY. Website: www.yorkcastlemuseum.org.uk